Philosophy for children

From child to children

Once upon a time!

Father in heaven protects us from all evil!

Coloring story!

By: Bernardo Octaviano Pereira

This book belongs to:

____

I dedicate this work, firstly, to my parents who I love so much, to my teachers, to my dear aunts and to all my friends, may God bless you all infinitely!

Bernardo Octaviano Pereira

16/04/2024

Once upon a time, in a place, near here, in a small town in the interior, where there was a little church, which had once been a scene of fervor and devotion, it was always very full;

But in recent times it has been emptying out, little by little, and almost no one was there anymore. On a certain festive night, it was drizzling and very fruitful, when the service began, no one had entered the little church;

And the preacher, faithful to his mission, waited, in the solitude of the altar, for the faithful to worship; Suddenly, an unexpected visitor entered the little church, a handsome man, well dressed and speaking very well;

And he told the preacher that people didn't want to go to little churches anymore, that they preferred to go to other places like bars, shopping malls, parties, especially on a cold, drizzling night, when no one would come in;

And the preacher asked who he was, and he replied that he was the bad animal; and he made a bet with the preacher, that if no one enters the little church that night, he would destroy everyone and everything in this little town;

And the preacher, confident in divine protection, accepted the challenge, knew that heavenly daddy would not let the bad creature win the bet, and destroy everything and everyone;

And time passed and no one came in, and the bad creature, laughing maliciously at the situation, announced his plan of destruction, saying that he would start with the little church with the preacher inside;

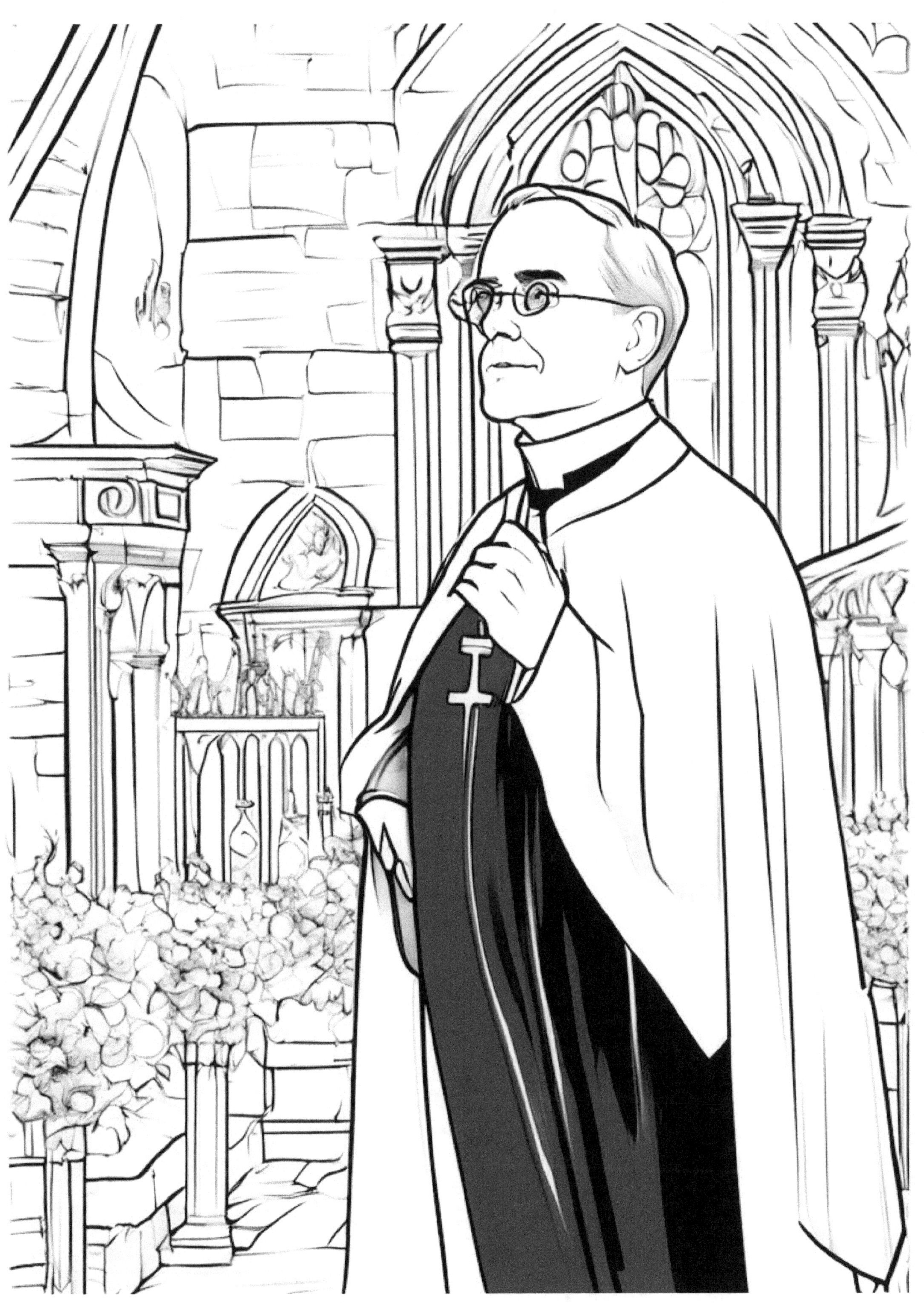

Then it would destroy the rest of the little town with everyone inside it, and almost at the end of the service a little boy came in, helpless and drenched in the rain, and he was very cold, and he went in to protect himself from the cold and the rain;

In the blink of an eye, the bad creature vanished into smoke and disappeared. The daddy in heaven, sending the little boy at the right time.

Havia frustrado os planos do bicho ruim. A fé e a esperança, representada por aquele inocente menino, provaram ser mais forte que qualquer mal.
He had thwarted the bad creature's plans. Faith and hope, represented by that innocent boy, proved to be stronger than any evil.

Thus, the small town learned a valuable lesson. Father in heaven protects us, often sending help in the most unexpected moments. We just need to trust and ask sincerely.

The end!